D1553381

The Pocket Book of Confidence

Illuminating the path to courage and self-belief

ARCTURUS

With special thanks to Anne Moreland

ARCTURUS

This edition published in 2016 by Arcturus Publishing Limited
26/27 Bickels Yard, 151–153 Bermondsey Street,
London SE1 3HA

ISBN: 978-1-78428-412-1
AD002245UK

Printed in China

Contents

Introduction

Everyone wants to be confident. We see people who seem to exude confidence, and wish we were like them. For confidence seems to bring with it so many benefits – success at work, in love, in friendship, and in countless other ways. Yet, when we start to think about it, we find ourselves asking, what is this elusive quality? What is true confidence? Where does it come from, and why do we so often feel that

we've lost it? Moreover, if we do lose it, how can we ever find it again?

This book brings together some ideas about confidence that will set you thinking. We look at how confidence is gained, first and foremost, through learning to value ourselves, through testing ourselves, and through rising to life's challenges. We also explore how we can 'talk ourselves' into being more confident. You will find here many quotations from famous writers, artists, sportspeople and others about finding the courage and determination to reach goals. And finally, you'll find some intriguing ideas about how having confidence remains a paradox that we human beings are constantly trying to solve.

What is Confidence?

What exactly do we mean by 'confidence'? Is it a characteristic we're born with, or do we learn it as we go through life? And how can we all agree on what this elusive but essential quality is?

Confidence is being sure of yourself; arrogance is having too high an opinion of yourself.

Believe in your ability, and you may find yourself being able to do greater things than you ever expected.

If you believe you'll fail, you'll be more likely to.

Accept yourself; then others will.

Confidence: optimism; self-esteem;
perseverance; respect for others;
a sense of responsibility; the ability to
apply oneself; faith in the future; and
a love of life.

Confidence is a habit that can be developed by acting as if you already have it!

Self-regard is the mainspring of all human activities.

François de La Rochefoucauld

A truly confident person is not unduly upset by failure. He or she will continue to value themselves whatever happens.

Trust, both in oneself and others, is the major part of confidence.

Appearance is everything. Feeling good about yourself on the outside will help you feel good on the inside.

Being free from the fear of failure means you can focus more clearly on what you're doing – and will be more likely to succeed.

15

Confident people listen
to criticism, but don't let
other people's opinion
define them.

Love all, trust a few. Do wrong to none.
William Shakespeare

For a child, knowing he or she is
loved unconditionally helps
to instil lifelong self-confidence
and a sense of security.

The sun doesn't need to remember to rise in the morning, or to set at night. Follow the sun, and live confidently, without thinking too much about it.

Our ancestors never crossed the sea and mapped the world by standing at the water's edge and wondering how deep and cold it was.

Character is higher than intellect.
Ralph Waldo Emerson

Confidence involves self-respect; knowing your rights and valuing yourself as a person.

An ounce of confidence is worth a pound of knowledge.

True confidence is about being able to compromise – letting others have their way when the situation demands.

A big smile and a firm handshake will tell people you are confident and comfortable with yourself.

Confidence is a stable sense of self-worth.

Believe that you can face the challenges of life; you have a right to pursue happiness.

The story of the human race is the story of men and women selling themselves short.

Abraham Maslow

A loved child will take it for granted that he or she is valued, and carry that confident feeling through to adulthood.

Loving others and loving yourself are two parts of the same whole.

Confidence is:

- believing in yourself
- holding core values
- trusting your own judgement
- learning from the past
- being open to change
- valuing others
- asking for help when you need it
- showing kindness to those around you
- standing up for yourself
- admitting when you are wrong
- liking yourself
- being kind to yourself when you fail

The curious paradox is that when I accept myself just as I am, then I can change.

Carl Rogers

If we allow others to disrespect us, we start to disrespect ourselves.

Boasting is a sign of insecurity. If you're confident, you don't need to point out to others how great you are!

Trust others, and you trust yourself.

Acknowledge your strengths, as well as your weaknesses, and value your uniqueness.

Confidence is understanding other people's emotions, as well as your own.

Being the first to extend the hand of friendship always involves the risk of rejection. If you're confident, you'll take that risk.

Gardens are not made by singing 'Oh how beautiful' and sitting in the shade.
Rudyard Kipling

In order to truly love another person,
you first need to love yourself.

Self-confidence is the key to happiness.

Inferiority is a state of mind in which you've declared yourself a victim.

Be comfortable with who you are.

It's good to be confident, but don't overestimate your abilities. Take a reality check now and then!

Act confident. By doing so, you'll find that, gradually, your confidence will increase.

Most of us waver between feeling confident and feeling afraid; as long as the confident side usually gains the upper hand, the balance will be about right.

Respect your efforts, respect yourself. Self-respect leads to self-discipline. When you have both firmly under your belt, that's real power. *Clint Eastwood*

Confidence is that feeling when you start out on a new project with optimism and trust in yourself.

Human beings need challenges. See them not as threats, but as opportunities to leave your comfort zone.

People gather bundles of sticks to build bridges they never cross.

Confidence is giving yourself credit where credit is due.

Don't focus on what you're bad at;
think about what you're good at,
and you'll find your estimation of
yourself goes up.

It's nice to be important. But it's more important to be nice.

The perfectionist cannot achieve his goals, and lives with a permanent sense of failure.

As is our confidence,
so is our capacity.
William Hazlitt

It is always possible to change your way of thinking and learn to respect yourself.

Real confidence isn't about brash behaviour; it's about being sensitive to other people's needs, without being overwhelmed by them.

Confidence is being prepared for any circumstances. Because circumstances are always outside your control.

As a member of the human race, you are equal to all other human beings in the world.
Never forget that.

Loving oneself is not about being selfish. It's about caring for oneself, taking responsibility, and being honest about one's capabilities.

The reckless confidence of the fool is not real confidence, but stupidity.

Those who trust themselves are always trusted.

No one can make you feel inferior without your consent.
Eleanor Roosevelt

Confidence is like a seed that needs to be nurtured, so that it grows.

Listening to constructive criticism is always a good idea. Learn from it, rather than taking it to heart and dwelling on it.

Confidence is your reward for overcoming fear.

Confidence is believing in yourself when no one else does.

Confidence is doing the things you cannot do.

Confidence is trusting your own instincts, not relying on other people to tell you how to behave.

Failure need not take everything away from you. You still have your confidence, your ability to bounce back.

Self-esteem is about showing the same respect and kindness to yourself as you would to a friend.

Confidence is that small, quiet voice that tells you 'Yes, you can'.

If you think you can, you can.

Confidence is a flat refusal to let fear get the better of us.

If you base your opinion of yourself entirely on what others think of you, you will never find true confidence.

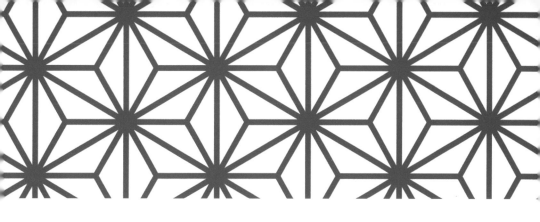

Fame and fortune does not build true confidence; being valued by those we love, and the community around us, does.

Look in the mirror every day and say out loud, 'I like myself'.

Compete with yourself, not with others.

Small acts of kindness help us to see ourselves as a positive force in the world, boosting our self-confidence.

Knowing how to give and take advice is a sign of confidence.

Confidence is about coping with the disappointments of life, as well as the successes.

Worry is a complete cycle of useless thought revolving around a pivot of fear.

Somebody is always doing what somebody else said couldn't be done.

Know who you really are. Then strive to be that person!

Patience is a sign of confidence; a belief that, eventually, a goal will be achieved, even if there are a few setbacks on the way.

Success comes in cans, not can'ts.

Worrying can be a lot harder work, and a lot more exhausting, than actually getting up and doing something about the problem you're worrying about.

Confidence is knowing yourself better than anyone else does.

Whether you think you can or think you can't – you are right. *Henry Ford*

Each time we face our fear, we gain strength, courage, and confidence in the doing.

Theodore Roosevelt

Treat yourself with respect, care, compassion, and tolerance. Be generous in forgiving your faults and mistakes.

I am convinced that all of humanity is born with more gifts than we know. Most are born geniuses and just get de-geniused rapidly.

Buckminster Fuller

Being confident is catching – if you show optimism and resolve in the face of difficulty, others around you will, too.

We all doubt; and we all have faith. Confidence is getting the right balance.

Loving the simple things of life makes it easier to be happy. And being happy brings confidence.

An umbrella can't stop the rain, but it can help us stay dry. Confidence is like the umbrella, shielding us from circumstance.

It takes courage to change. But change we must, for all around us changes.

Every small task accomplished, every great goal achieved, brings us confidence.

To whistle and sing for pure joy, on a beautiful day,

is an act of confidence in the wonder of life.

Don't try to be a 'people pleaser'. You'll never be able to please everyone, and you'll probably annoy your friends and family in the process!

You can measure a person's confidence by what it takes to discourage them.

Confident people do not bully others. Bullies are insecure people who are afraid to let others have their own way.

Don't ask yourself, Why? Ask yourself, Why not?

If you doubt yourself, then indeed you stand on shaky ground.
Henrik Ibsen

There are limits in life, and the confident person soon learns what they are.

It takes time and effort to be
confident. Start by recognizing
that you are a good person,
worthy of love and respect.

**Fear holds us back.
Confidence drives us forward.**

Confidence is having the strength of
mind to say 'no' when other people
make unreasonable demands on you.

It's not who you
are that holds you
back, it's who you
think you're not.

Drag your thoughts away from your troubles. By the ears, by the heels, or any other way you can manage it.
Mark Twain

Skill and confidence are an unbeatable partnership.

To undermine a man's self-respect is a sin.
Antoine de Saint-Exupéry

Confidence is a combination of self-belief, an understanding of the situation one finds oneself in, and an ability to set to work to put things right.

Confidence isn't just about being optimistic. It's about being realistic, too, and determined to do your best whatever the circumstances.

Gaining Confidence

There are many ways to achieve confidence: through support from others, and through our own achievements whether in work or in love and friendship. But it doesn't come overnight; and we all have to start somewhere.

To the optimist, all
that exists holds the
potential for beauty.

Mistakes are not always
the mark of laziness.
Sometimes, they reveal
ambition, originality,
and a desire to do better.

To thine own self be true
And it must follow as the night the day
Thou canst not then be false to any man.
William Shakespeare

Some of us are born confident. But most of us learn how to be, through rising to the challenges of life.

Don't bottle up your feelings. Of course, we sometimes have to hide our emotions, but it's important to express yourself honestly whenever you can.

Too much confidence is the harbinger of danger.

If you're confident, you will expect your partner, close family, and friends to understand when you express your doubts and difficulties in life.

Resentment is the enemy of confidence, for hatred eats away at the self.

The gain in self-confidence at having accomplished a tiresome labour is immense. *Arnold Bennett*

Don't praise others just to give them confidence. If they've not done well, just tell them that next time, you know they'll do better.

Being sulky or resentful doesn't get you anywhere. If you're not happy about something, have the confidence to say so, as politely as you can.

The reputation of a thousand years may be determined by the conduct of one hour.
Japanese proverb

If you rely on the opinion of others to give you confidence, you're bound to fail.

Confidence is the finest gift that we can hope to bring our children, for it allows them to choose their own path in life.

We all encounter dominating people who want to push us around. Stand up to them, quietly and firmly. If you get angry instead, you risk losing your moral ground and, sometimes, the battle.

If I have lost confidence in myself, I have the universe against me.
Ralph Waldo Emerson

My aim in life is to be as good a person as my dog thinks I am.

Optimism is expecting the best; confidence, knowing how to handle the worst.

Trouble is part of life. When it confronts you, look it straight in the eye and let it know that it cannot defeat you.

The best way to stand up to a bully is to:

- know your facts, so you can defend your position
- think about what will happen in advance, so you're prepared
- ask thoughtful, open questions
- behave in a strong, firm manner
- practise controlling your fear
- feel sympathy for, rather than fear of, their weakness

Persons with weight of character carry, like planets, their atmospheres along with them in their orbits.

Thomas Hardy

Don't dwell on what may go wrong. It won't help the outcome of your endeavour, or your general confidence.

When you criticize others, say, 'I feel...' rather than 'You are...'. That way, you're stating your personal position rather than making a judgement.

Attempt easy tasks as if they were difficult, and difficult as if they were easy; in the one case that confidence may not fall asleep, in the other that it may not be dismayed. ***Baltasar Gracián***

If you feel angry, recognize it; only then will you begin to learn how to control it.

In times of trouble, we all need to talk. Find a close friend or family member and tell them how you feel.

I am, indeed, a king, because I know how to rule myself.
Pietro Aretino

You can't change the past, so instead learn to accept it, and what you perceive as your mistakes.

In order to feel a failure, you have to ignore your successes.

Have faith, for everything on the earth has a purpose; every disease a herb to cure; and every person a mission.
Native American proverb

Becoming a confident person is setting out on a voyage of discovery.

Remember that other people are not always as confident as they look.
They have their own problems, too. They may just be better at hiding them.

81

Give yourself permission to take pride in yourself: your talents, skills, experience, likeable qualities… the list goes on…

Bowing to another's will good-humouredly, where the matter is not important, is a sure sign of confidence.

Focus on what you have, rather than what you lack.

In matters of principle, stand like a rock; in matters of taste, swim with the current.
Thomas Jefferson

Don't immediately respond to compliments with a negative comment about yourself. Learn to accept them gracefully when they come.

Set yourself some challenges. Even if you don't succeed, you'll feel better for trying.

Money, beauty, and fame are not the only indicators of success. Recognize them as shallow, and look for deeper meaning in life.

Exercise and good diet is a great confidence booster. When you're feeling healthy, you feel happier about yourself, and it will show.

Don't bother just to be better than your contemporaries or predecessors. Try to be better than yourself. *William Faulkner*

When you express yourself creatively, whether through writing, music, dance, or art, you build your confidence as a person… whatever the results.

Taking responsibility for yourself is part of being a confident adult.

Think of yourself as successful. It doesn't always come naturally, but there is no reason why you shouldn't be proud of yourself and your achievements in life.

The quickest route to giving a person confidence is to love them.

Don't put yourself down. A negative way of talking about yourself, even when you're joking, will start to affect the way you think about yourself.

Confidence is not always about trying harder. Sometimes, it's about enjoying the moment, secure in the knowledge that we are fine just as we are.

You can't connect the dots looking forward, you can only connect them looking backwards. So you have to trust that the dots will somehow connect in your future. You have to trust in something: your gut, destiny, life, karma, whatever. Because believing that the dots will connect down the road will give you the confidence to follow your own heart, even when it leads you off the well-worn path. *Steve Jobs*

Only insecure people always have to have their own way. To speak ill of others is a dishonest way of praising ourselves.
Will Durant

Don't dither when making decisions. It's a sign that you are overly concerned about failure.

Confidence is the force that drives you towards your dream.

When demands are made on you, weigh up whether they're fair or not before you respond.

Education is the ability to listen to anything without losing your temper or your self-confidence. *Robert Frost*

Love is a form of confidence: an unshakeable belief in, and respect for, the one you love, irrespective of their weaknesses and strengths.

Every one of us is born confident enough to cry out and demand attention. Not all of us keep that confidence for life… but you can be sure that somewhere, deep down, it still remains.

Don't let other people make decisions for you. If you allow them to, you'll find yourself resentful that they're running your life.

We are often afraid to be openly confident for fear of seeming conceited. But there's a big difference between singing your own praises and being calmly sure of yourself.

Confidence and willpower march together, hand in hand.

Making firm decisions and sticking to them is a great confidence-booster. Even if you make mistakes, you will feel more in control of your life.

Don't let other people's opinion of you – real or imagined – affect your self-confidence. Only you really know yourself and the circumstances of your life.

When you feel insecure, ask yourself the following questions:

- What have I learned from my life experiences?
- What are my strong points as a person?
- What talents do I have?
- What skills have I developed?
- What do I enjoy doing?

Then ask yourself how you can build on these positive elements.

Don't be too quick to judge others.
Each person has their own story,
which is one that you probably
know very little about.

Confidence is less a quality; more, an unknown quantity.

Listen to others, but when it's your turn, speak up for yourself.

Every great achievement starts with the decision to try, and the confidence to act.

True confidence springs from knowing that, whatever happens, you'll do your best to cope.

When the going gets tough, the tough get going.

Don't blame yourself for bad luck or difficult circumstances. Instead, pat yourself on the back for persevering when times get tough.

Be courteous to all, and intimate with few, and let those few be well tried before you give them your confidence.

George Washington

Blaming someone else for your problems implies that they have more control over the situation than you do. Ask yourself, is that really true?

Common sense and confidence
make good companions.

**Sometimes
being confident
is more
important than
being right.**

Peace is not an absence of war; it is a virtue, a state of mind, a disposition for benevolence, confidence, justice.
Spinoza

It is not so much our friends' help that helps us, as the confidence of their help. *Epicurus*

Being confident means taking responsibility. You – and no one else – are the person in control of your approach to life, your behaviour, and your emotions. So don't dodge the task!

Shyness does not always denote lack of confidence. Sometimes, quiet people have a strong sense of their own self-worth, but don't feel the need to brag about it.

Nothing ventured, nothing gained.

Kindness in words creates confidence.
Kindness in thought creates wisdom.
Kindness in giving creates love.
Lao Tzu

If we are lucky enough to be blessed with a family that gives us unconditional love, we will grow in confidence every day.

Without confidence, perseverance
is impossible.

**For they conquer who
believe they can.**
John Dryden

Courage is wanting to do well. Security is knowing you can do well. Confidence is having done well.

There are always other people to blame for the problems in life. Don't spend time analyzing their faults; instead, focus on what you can do to put things right.

When you feel mistreated and misunderstood, you may be tempted to play the martyr. Don't. Chances are, no one will notice you suffering in silence.

Is life not a hundred times too short to stifle ourselves. *Friedrich Nietzsche*

Two steps forward, one step back. Thus, slowly, we make progress.

Confidence is the bond of friendship.
Publilius Syrus

Our self-worth shouldn't be based on how much money we earn, and how important our position is.

Grasping opportunities when they come along is a sign of self-confidence and willingness to challenge oneself.

No one ever feels confident all the time. So have some coping strategies when you feel insecure.

There can never be complete confidence in a power which is excessive. *Tacitus*

As we go through life, we naturally learn, through experience, what we can do, and what we can't. But we have to make a conscious effort to focus on the 'can', rather than the 'can't'.

Generalized thinking, such as 'Things always go wrong for me', is the enemy of self-confidence. Remind yourself that one setback doesn't mean total failure.

Try not to bury your head in the sand when it comes to money. Even if your resources are limited, think about how you can best use them to create a secure future for yourself.

A good meal, a hot bath, and settling down in bed with a good book can do wonders to restore confidence after a difficult day.

No one can steal your dreams. They belong to you, and only you.

No one goes through life without any difficulties. But some people manage to develop more resilience than others – that is, they learn how to take the knocks and carry on regardless.

Everybody grows old. Not everybody grows up.

Confidence contributes more to conversation than wit.

François de la Rochefoucauld

When somebody asks you what you do for a living, respond positively. Don't say you're 'just a' this or that. If you do, the message will be that you don't really value yourself.

Don't live down to other people's expectations of you; live up to your own.

Do you take people as you find them, regardless of appearance, social status, culture or class? If you can honestly say yes, you are a person who has confidence in their own judgement, rather than that of society.

Honest, constructive criticism from a loved one may sometimes hurt, but if you listen and learn, it can help build, rather than ruin, your confidence.

Confidence is valuing your time. Think about how you would ideally balance your life between work, family, and other demands, including time for yourself. Then work towards creating that balance.

Confidence in the face of the unknown is a requirement for the creative process.

If you want something really badly, you must work to achieve it. And in the process, you may find that the work is what drives you.

Life isn't a matter of finding yourself. It's more to do with creating yourself.

I am not a has-been. I am a will-be.

Being confident means not being afraid to show your vulnerability to those you love, and those who love you.

Teach your children to respect authority, not to live in fear of it.

Laugh at yourself when things go wrong; it'll help you regain your confidence.

We are what we pretend to be, so we must be careful what we pretend to be. *Kurt Vonnegut*

Make time for what you really care about in life. Whatever other people tell you, it is you that must decide how you want to live.

Always be a first-rate version of yourself, not a second-rate version of somebody else.
Judy Garland

Try to live in the present, not the past, or the future. You'll have more fun, and feel more confident as a person, without the weight of regret or expectation on your shoulders.

The best way to become confident is to tackle what you're scared of.

You don't have to have the right qualifications in order to apply for the job of being who you want to be.

We are betrayed by what is false within.
George Meredith

More important than the will to win is the confidence to begin.

The confident person must be prepared to face rejection over and over again, whether in love or at work, because without this ability nothing can be achieved or even attempted.

If you want to give advice, be prepared to take it, too.

We don't always know how to define confidence, but we always recognize it when we see it in a person: through a gesture, a smile, a word… in short, by watching the way he carries himself.

Confidence is a matter of knowing what you expect from life, as well as what life expects from you.

We turn not older with years, but newer every day. *Emily Dickinson*

The Guides

Wise words from those who have achieved much in their time, and who come from all walks of life, from poets and philosophers to stars of stage and screen. And some handy hints from the anonymous voices of history, too.

If you hear a voice within you say 'you cannot paint', then by all means paint, and that voice will be silenced.

Vincent Van Gogh

The pillar of the world is hope.
African proverb

Make the most of yourself, for that is all there is of you.
Ralph Waldo Emerson

Knock the 't' off the 'can't'.

It is not the mountain we conquer, but ourselves. *Edmund Hillary*

If you put a low value on yourself, you can't expect others to raise the price.

Great tranquillity of the heart is his who cares for neither praise nor blame. *Thomas à Kempis*

I am not afraid of storms for I am learning how to sail my ship.

Louisa May Alcott

Where there is no enemy within, the enemies outside cannot hurt you.
African proverb

Put your future in good hands – your own.

I have a key in my bosom, called Promise, that will, I am persuaded, open any lock in Doubting Castle.
John Bunyan

A lotta cats copy the Mona Lisa, but people still line up to see the original.
Louis Armstrong

There are limitations in life, but most of them you set yourself.

Never dull your shine for somebody else.
Tyra Banks

Don't worry about what people will think of you. Most of the time, they will be thinking about themselves.

Insist on yourself; never imitate.
Ralph Waldo Emerson

Choose a job you love, and you will never have to work a day in your life. *Confucius*

When you're moving in the positive, your destination is the brightest star.
Stevie Wonder

Regardless of how you feel inside, always try to look like a winner. Even if you are behind, a sustained look of control and confidence can give you a mental edge that results in victory. *Arthur Ashe*

Only by accepting yourself will you be accepted by others.

The best way to gain self-confidence is to do what you are afraid to do.

If you're trying to achieve, there will be roadblocks. I've had them; everybody has had them. But obstacles don't have to stop you. If you run into a wall, don't turn around and give up. Figure out how to climb it, go through it, or work around it. *Michael Jordan*

We do not walk on our legs, but on our will.
Sufi proverb

Sex appeal is fifty per cent what you've got, and fifty per cent what people think you've got.

Sophia Loren

Our doubts are traitors
And make us lose the good we oft might win
By fearing to attempt.
William Shakespeare

It is folly for a man to pray to the gods for that which he has the power to obtain by himself.
Epicurus

Building a child's self-confidence starts from the earliest days, by being sensitive to your baby's needs.

Confidence comes when you show yourself the same love that you show others.

To wish you were someone else is to waste the person you are.
Sven Göran Eriksson

Always behave as if you're wearing an invisible crown.

Anyone who ever gave you
confidence, you owe them a lot.
Truman Capote

Don't bemoan what you are not; value what you are.

Always hold your head up, but be careful to keep your nose at a friendly level. *Max L. Forman*

A good leader inspires people to have confidence in him. A great leader inspires people to have confidence in themselves. *Lao Tzu*

Just as much as we see in others we have in ourselves. *William Hazlitt*

All you need in this life is ignorance and confidence; then success is sure. *Mark Twain*

If you think you're too small to make a difference, try going to bed with a mosquito in the room.

Some of your griefs you have cured.
And the sharpest you still have survived,
But what torments of pain you endured.
From evils that never arrived.
Ralph Waldo Emerson

Only by knowing your own power will you become powerful.

If my mind can conceive it and my heart can believe it, I know I can achieve it.

Jesse Jackson

Life is not easy for any of us. But what of that? We must have perseverance and, above all, confidence in ourselves. We must believe that we are gifted for something and that this thing, at whatever cost, must be attained.
Marie Curie

Wellbeing and confidence comes from a deep sense of attachment to others.

I was always looking outside myself for confidence and strength, but it comes from within. It is there all the time.
Anna Freud

Don't let fear of other people's jealousy hold you back from shining brightly, like a star.

Without a humble but reasonable confidence in your own powers you cannot be successful or happy.
Norman Vincent Peale

Your real boss is the one who walks around under your hat. *Napoleon Hill*

Chiefly the mould of a man's fortune is in his own hands.
Francis Bacon

Look in the mirror, and like the person you see.

Impossible is just a big word thrown around by small men who find it easier to live in the world they've been given than to explore the power they have to change it. Impossible is not a fact. It's an opinion. Impossible is not a declaration. It's a dare. Impossible is potential. Impossible is temporary. Impossible is nothing.

David Beckham

The secret of success is to believe in yourself. After that, everything else follows.

Be modest, but don't hold a low opinion of yourself.

A great deal of talent is lost to the world for want of a little courage.
Sydney Smith

As you become more clear about who you really are, you'll be better able to decide what is best for you – the first time around.
Oprah Winfrey

Confront your fears. It is the only way to achieve confidence in life.

You don't need a degree in psychology to bring up a confident child.

Far more important than other people's assessment of you is the assessment you make of yourself.

Self-assurance is fatal unless it is self-knowledge. *George Santayana*

My theory is that if you look confident you can pull off anything – even if you have no clue what you're doing.
Jessica Alba

Confidence …
thrives on honesty,
on honour, on
the sacredness of
obligations, on
faithful protection,
and on unselfish
performance. Without
them, it cannot live.

Franklin D. Roosevelt

Confidence in the goodness of another is good proof of one's own goodness.

Michel de Montaigne

If you don't feel confident, just try to look as though you do.

When you reach the top, keep climbing.

Self-confidence is the first requisite to great undertakings.

I quit being afraid when my first venture failed and the sky didn't fall down.

Allen H. Neuharth

Peace of mind follows when you make a decision, even if it isn't always the right decision.

We are each gifted in a unique and important way. It is our privilege and our adventure to discover our own special light.
Mary Dunbar

Never bend your head. Always hold it high. Look the world straight in the face. *Helen Keller*

Recognize your child's special talents, and then nurture them to build his or her confidence as a whole person.

Confidence is what you have before you understand the problem.
Woody Allen

Most of the shadows in this life are caused by standing in one's own sunshine.
Ralph Waldo Emerson

Don't compare yourself with others.
You are unique.

A wise man makes his own decisions.
An ignorant man follows public opinion.
Chinese proverb

It's not what you think you are that holds you back. It's what you think you're not.

Confidence helps us deal with the negative effects of everyday stress.

It ain't what they call you, it's what you answer to. *W.C. Fields*

Those who are silent, self-effacing, and attentive become the recipients of confidences. *Thornton Wilder*

Most of the confidence which I appear to feel, especially when influenced by noon wine, is only a pretence.
Tennessee Williams

Most of us, as we get older, gain rather than lose confidence in ourselves.

I am not interested in money. I just want to be wonderful.

Marilyn Monroe

A bird does not sing because it has an answer. It sings because it has a song. *Chinese proverb*

Don't run yourself down, especially in front of your children – they will learn that you have low self-esteem, and may copy you.

Let us never negotiate out of fear but let us never fear to negotiate.
John F. Kennedy

A man cannot be comfortable without his own approval.
Mark Twain

Give praise whenever you can, but only when praise is due.
We are each gifted in a unique and important way. It is our privilege and our adventure to discover our own special light.
Mary Dunbar

If you try to reassure others, you will help to reassure yourself.
If I have the belief that I can do it, I shall surely acquire the capacity to do it even if I may not have it at the beginning.
Mahatma Gandhi

A dream you dream alone is only a dream. A dream you dream together is reality.
John Lennon

The worst fear we have is lack of belief in ourselves.

By being yourself, you put something wonderful in the world that was not there before.
Edwin Elliot

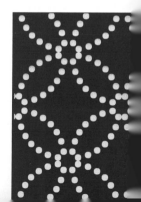

The only thing we have to fear is fear itself.
Franklin D. Roosevelt

Health is the greatest possession, contentment the greatest treasure, and confidence the greatest friend. *Lao Tzu*

Laugh with others – not at them.

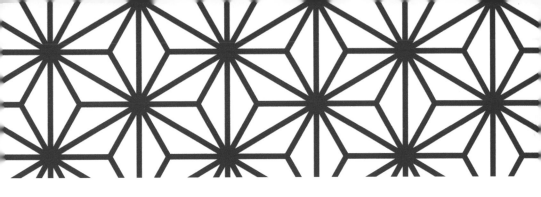

Try not to label yourself, or the people you love. Instead, see them as personalities that are constantly changing and growing.

We are not won by arguments that we can analyze, but by tone and temper; by the manner, which is the man himself. *Samuel Butler*

An optimist is a person who sees a green light everywhere; while a pessimist sees only the red stop light. The truly wise person is colour blind.

Albert Schweitzer

By mutual confidence and mutual aid Great deeds are done, and great discoveries made. *Homer*

It is much easier to see the weaknesses in ourselves than the strengths. That's because we know ourselves only too well.

Confidence imparts a wonderful inspiration to its possessor.
John Milton

Confidence is the hinge on the door to success.
Wally Amos

Confidence is a balance between expressing and controlling emotions.

I learned that courage was not the absence of fear, but the triumph over it. The brave man is not he who does not feel afraid, but he who conquers fear.
Nelson Mandela

Always blaming yourself is egocentric. Remember, the world doesn't revolve around you.

All things splendid have been achieved by those who dared believe that something inside them was superior to circumstance. *Bruce Barton*

If at first you do succeed, try something harder.

Nothing builds self-esteem and self-confidence like accomplishment.
Thomas Carlyle

People are like stained-glass windows. They sparkle and shine when the sun is out, but when the darkness sets in, their true beauty is revealed only if there is light from within.

Elisabeth Kübler-Ross

Everybody is a genius. But if you judge a fish by its ability to climb a tree, it will spend its whole life believing that it is stupid. *Albert Einstein*

Of all our infirmities, the most savage is to despise our being.
Michel de Montaigne

Criticize behaviour, not your child.

Self-confidence is the first requisite to great undertakings.
Samuel Johnson

There is one blessing only, the source and cornerstone of beatitude: confidence in self. *Seneca*

Personality is the glitter that sends your little gleam across the footlights and the orchestra pit into that big black space where the audience is.

Mae West

Smile, for everyone lacks confidence and, more than any other one thing, a smile reassures them.
André Maurois

Meet people's gaze openly and honestly. That way, you will give an impression of confidence.

Almost everyone feels insecure sometimes. Part of self-confidence is knowing that, and being sensitive to the needs of others.

Smooth seas do not make skilful sailors.

187

If you have no confidence in self, you are twice defeated in the race of life. With confidence, you have won even before you have started. *Marcus Garvey*

Good judgement comes from experience, and experience from bad judgement.

Better keep yourself clean and bright; you are the window through which you see the world.

George Bernard Shaw

Confidence is that feeling by which the mind embarks on great and honourable courses with a sure hope and trust in itself. *Cicero*

Once we believe in ourselves, we can risk curiosity, wonder, spontaneous delight, or any experience that reveals the human spirit. *E.E. Cummings*

Confidence comes from being loved and respected for who you are. It's a gift we get from others, and one that we learn to give ourselves.

Trust Yourself

Trusting yourself is the first step on the road to confidence. That means taking a clear look at your strengths, so that you can build on them; and recognizing your weaknesses, so you can begin to change and accommodate them.

We all need our comfort zone, but if we stay in it too long, we risk becoming lazy, timid, and unadventurous.

Listen to others, but trust your own judgement. In the end, it's you who must decide how to live your life.

Assurance is two-thirds of success.

Try to put others at ease. Show interest in their lives, just as you would hope they would show interest in yours.

When we stop thinking about how we feel, we start to think about how others feel, which is the beginning of trust.

Trusting yourself doesn't mean avoiding mistakes; it means knowing that, one way or another, you will be able to learn from them and continue to move forward.

'C' is for Courage
'O' is for Overcoming
'N' is for Nonchalance
'F' is for Fearlessness
'I' is for Integrity
'D' is for Determination
'E' is for Energy
'N' is for No Fear
'C' is for Clarity
'E' is for Endeavour

It's better to know some of the questions than all of the answers.

James Thurber

Time spent alone, pursuing activities that you enjoy, is an important part of building a confident personality.

The biggest step is the one you take to go outside your front door every day.

Believe in your values and principles. Defend them when you find opposition, but be confident enough to change them when experience shows you are wrong.

Honesty is telling other people the truth. Integrity is telling yourself the truth.

Strangers are just friends you haven't met yet.

The trusting man may be fooled now and again, but he will live a fuller, happier life than the man who doubts everyone and everything.

To begin your journey on the path to confidence, you need to trust yourself. That doesn't mean assuming that you're always right, or that things will go well, but simply having faith in yourself as a powerful person with the resources to cope with the challenges life brings.

Making safety your first priority in life can be a way of building a prison for yourself. Of course, we need to feel safe; but we also need to throw caution to the winds, sometimes, and live a little.

Valuing yourself gives you confidence and self-respect.

To tell a lie, you need to be afraid of something or someone. To tell the truth, you must have confidence in something or someone.

There's no greater fraud than a promise not kept.

Take a chance! All life is a chance. The man who goes the furthest is generally the one who is willing to do and dare. The 'sure thing' boat never gets far from shore.

Dale Carnegie

How do we know when to trust a person? It's partly to do with the confidence, or lack of it, that they display in themselves.

If you can't find the job you want – create it. Even if it has to run alongside your other job for a while, it will bring confidence and creativity into your life.

I am always doing that which I cannot do, in order that I may learn how to do it. *Pablo Picasso*

When people trust you, they place their confidence in you. And that's a great compliment.

Being too modest about oneself is a form of pride masquerading as humility.

It does not matter how slowly you go, as long as you do not stop.

Confucius

There is nothing noble in being superior to others. True nobility lies in being superior to your former self.

There's no need to change your behaviour in order to 'fit in' with what others expect of you. Instead, consider how you treat others, and how you treat yourself, so you can become a better person.

Asking for advice is not a sign that you lack confidence. Rather, it may show that you have respect for other people's opinions, and the confidence to admit that you don't know everything.

Money, sex, power, success, and beauty all bring great thrills. But they don't last long if inner confidence is missing.

Hard work is our business; its success is out of our hands.

Dress confidently, to present yourself well and reveal the person you are, or would like to be.

However confident we are, it is always something of a surprise when we achieve our goals. And a cause for delighted celebration!

To dare is to lose one's footing momentarily. Not to dare is to lose oneself. *Søren Kierkegaard*

Socializing is a matter of understanding that other people may be feeling shy and uncomfortable, and putting them at their ease. If you do that, you'll forget about any feelings of shyness yourself.

Nothing in the world can take the place of Persistence. Talent will not; nothing is more common than unsuccessful men with talent. Genius will not; unrewarded genius is almost a proverb. Education will not; the world is full of educated derelicts. Persistence and Determination alone are omnipotent.

Calvin Coolidge

He who has never tasted what is bitter does not know what is sweet.

Inflated self-esteem can lead to many problems, including expecting too much of life, having an unrealistic idea of one's own capabilities, and being angry when things go wrong.

215

Having too much confidence in others is foolish; but having no confidence in them is perhaps even more so.

Trust isn't something you're born with. It's something you achieve.

True confidence comes from starting out with a positive attitude, testing one's abilities, learning from experience, and continuing, whatever the difficulties in life, to move forward.

Confidence is about valuing yourself. Not above others, or below; but simply, as a unique, lovable human being, with your own special talents, skills, strengths, and weaknesses.

If you want to win, you must be prepared to lose.

Learn from the past; plan for the future; but live in the present.

Admit and accept your faults and failings; try to remedy them; then forget about them, and move on.

You are equal in dignity to any other human being on the planet, whatever their income, talent, skill, or social position.

Self-esteem is a basic human need; without it, we cannot develop in a healthy, normal way, or thrive in the social world around us.

If you take credit for other people's work, you show that you are a weak person who needs to impress, by whatever means. That isn't confidence; it's lack of confidence.

Widen your capacity to be confident; understand that you deserve to be confident; and, by so doing, you will help yourself to be confident.

Acceptance; love; respect. These are the building blocks of confidence.

Optimism; benevolence; endeavour. These are the outward signs of confidence.

As a cure for worrying, work is better than whiskey.
Thomas Edison

Those with high self-esteem feel confident and capable.
Those with low self-esteem feel fearful and overwhelmed.
Those in the middle, like most of us, waver between the two states.

Contrary to what many believe, a confident person does not go through life being cheerfully insensitive to the feelings of others. True confidence consists in being thoughtful about other people's needs, as well as your own.

For peace of mind, resign as general manager of the universe.

223

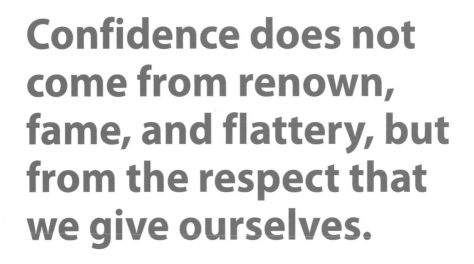

Confidence does not come from renown, fame, and flattery, but from the respect that we give ourselves.

In close relationships, confident people find it easier to forgive than those who lack confidence.

If you trust your own judgement, you won't be upset when others dislike the choice you've made; neither will you keep worrying about whether you made the right choice.

Self-confidence comes from believing in yourself: discovering and celebrating what you can do in the world – and doing it!

The Path to Self-Esteem

Many of us grow up with low self-esteem, either because of negative childhood experiences, difficult circumstances, or complex personality traits. Leraning to value yourself is important to becoming self-confident, and it's not as difficult as it may sound; much of what's required means simply changing your perspective.

Being loved

Being liked

Being listened to

Being respected

Being encouraged

Being helped when things go wrong…

All of this builds confidence and

self-esteem.

Our remedies oft in ourselves do lie, Which we ascribe to heaven. *William Shakespeare*

Nothing reduces the odds against you like ignoring them. ***Robert Brault***

The first time you try and fail, you think the world will end. Then it doesn't, which gives you the confidence to try again.

A touchy person will always take offence at a tactless remark; a confident one will assume that the person making it was mistaken.

People with low self-esteem find it difficult to deal with conflict. Either they give in, or they expect people to agree with every word they say. Confident people know that conflict is inescapable, and with patience and kindness, can be resolved.

We always have a distorted view of ourselves. The things we regard as weaknesses may actually be strengths, and what we like about ourselves may not be as important to others as we think.

When facing a big challenge in life: prepare for it, by talking yourself through the anxieties; confront it, through meeting it head-on, with determination and perseverance; and afterwards, when you've survived it, sit back and reflect on what you've learned.

All of us have wonders hidden in our breasts, only needing circumstances to evoke them. *Charles Dickens*

If there is no enemy within you, you can face all manner of challenges in life.

Never esteem anything as of advantage to you that will make you break your word or lose your self-respect. *Marcus Aurelius*

What you are to yourself is more important than what you are to others. Only by recognizing this can you become an independent person.

There's nothing wrong with being sad sometimes. Life is full of difficulties, and it's hard to be cheerful all the time. But it's when we get lost in sadness, and won't let it go, that we need to stop and think about why our confidence has begun to disappear.

What a man thinks of himself, that is what determines, or rather indicates, his fate.
Henry David Thoreau

Men are not against you; they are only for themselves. *Gene Fowler*

Little things can boost our confidence so much. A trip to the hairdresser; a new outfit; a chat with a close friend over coffee or lunch; phoning a friend we haven't seen for ages. These may seem insignificant, but they can make the difference between a dull day and a bright one.

Only by self-respect will you compel others to respect you.
Fyodor Dostoevsky

Every time people say things you find hurtful, put yourself in their shoes, and ask yourself why they might have said that. You'll realize that their remarks spring from their own insecurity, and are nothing to do with you.

If you're very shy, ask yourself, why am I always thinking about me, and the impression I make on other people? It could be that, in actual fact, nobody pays a great deal of attention to you, and you can't admit that to yourself.

It's easy to be confident when things are going well, or when you choose the easy path. Far harder when bad luck strikes, or you decide to aim high and risk failure. That's when you need to trust your instincts, to help you through the hard times.

Self-esteem is not fixed; your ideas about yourself can change, whether as a result of bitter experience, or, more positively, because you take a long, hard look at some of your deeply held beliefs and opinions about the person you are, and begin to question them.

When you come to the end of your rope, tie a knot and hang on!

Franklin D. Roosevelt

We are often afraid to express our feelings because we think they're irrational. Don't be. No one can help the way they feel, only the way they behave.

Don't hate yourself. Just stop listening to the part of yourself that hates yourself.

If you know you have done your best, it is easier to walk away from a situation without guilt or self-recrimination.

Dreams can guide us to where we want to go. But they can't take us there. In reality, it is up to us to make our dreams come true.

Self-respect cannot be bought, but it can easily be sold.

Respect yourself and others will respect you. *Buddha*

What is self-esteem? Perhaps that special feeling when we have achieved a goal, and know that in some deep, important way, we have come into our own – that is, realized our true potential.

A little man often casts a long shadow.
Italian proverb

In early years, basic ideas about one's personality are being formed.

Our ordinary mind always tries to persuade us that we are nothing but acorns and that our greatest happiness will be to become bigger, fatter, shinier acorns; but that is of interest only to pigs. Our faith gives us knowledge of something better: that we can become oak trees. *E.F. Schumacher*

To be truly confident, you need to have realistic expectations in life. Aim high, but make sure you keep a sense of proportion. Otherwise, you're bound to disappoint yourself.

Discipline weighs ounces; regret weighs tons.

Tell yourself each morning, as you look in the mirror, 'Every day, in every way, I'm getting better and better'.

Some days there won't be a song in your heart. Sing, anyway. *Emory Austin*

If passion drives you, let reason hold the reins.
Benjamin Franklin

When your dreams turn to dust, take out the broom, get to work, and sweep up.

Low self-esteem is based on opinions, not facts. And most of the opinions are your own, not other people's. So it's possible to change them.

Money and power can bring confidence; but so, too, can living responsibly in a sustainable way; trying to be open, honest, and kind as a person; and enjoying sharing the gifts of the planet fairly with your fellow human beings.

The difference between perseverance and obstinacy is that one comes from a strong will, and the other from a strong won't.
Henry Ward Beecher

Attitude is a little thing that makes a big difference.
Winston Churchill

Make a list of things you like about yourself: your characteristics; your looks; your kind or thoughtful actions; your skills. You'll find that you have a whole lot to offer.

Loving relationships with others are essential to our sense of self-worth. And knowing that your love and support is essential to another's wellbeing is also crucial.

I have no right, by anything I do or say, to demean a human being in his own eyes. What matters is not what I think of him; it is what he thinks of himself.

Antoine de Saint-Exupéry

Think about how friends, family, and acquaintances make you feel. Spend more time with the ones who make you feel good about yourself, and less with the ones who make you feel bad. It's as simple as that!

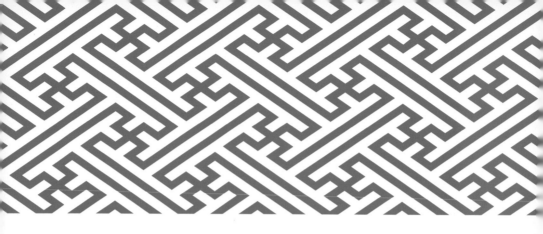

Finding time to do the things you love to do – whether walking by the sea, pottering around the garden, visiting museums and art galleries – nurtures the soul, opens your eyes to the beauties of the world, and makes you feel a better person.

You only have one life on earth; live it to the full, with faith, trust, confidence, and love.

The drops of rain make a hole in the stone not by violence but by oft falling. *Lucretius*

Being assertive is not a matter of being aggressive or difficult; it is to do with expressing your feelings if you've been upset, and being able to turn down unreasonable requests in a confident, open manner.

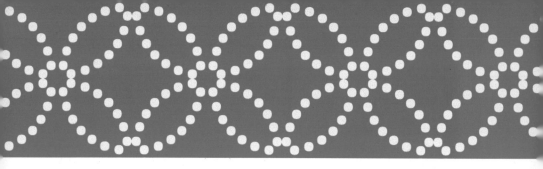

Don't wait passively for something to happen.
Be proactive – go out and make it happen!

Vitality is shown not only in the ability to persist but in the ability to start over. *F. Scott Fitzgerald*

We can't tell the wind which way to blow, but we can trim the sails so that we make the most of it.

Surround yourself with objects you love: pictures, photographs, knick, knacks that you've kept for years, home-made gifts given to you by children. They are outward signs of a well-lived life, and will cheer you in times of trouble.

Don't be afraid to give your best to what seemingly are small jobs. Every time you conquer one it makes you that much stronger. If you do the little jobs well, the big ones will tend to take care of themselves. *Dale Carnegie*

Finding the Way

We can't always be confident all the time. That's our nature as human beings. But we can find ways to keep on track, so that after a setback we can begin to build our confidence again, and continue to move forward in our lives.

Confidence is: self-esteem; optimism; courage; integrity; the ability to trust oneself, and to trust others; an understanding of one's capabilities; and the energy to fulfil one's potential.

To reassure, speak in a quiet, firm tone of voice; to inspire, use an enthusiastic one. Both will let the listener know you are a confident person, who means what you say.

Confidence is another word for concentration: the ability to keep your mind on the task in hand, not allowing yourself to become distracted by the feeling that you may fail.

When you feel afraid, think back to a time when you felt happy and confident. What has changed since then? You can't go back, so carry some of that feeling forward, into your present situation.

259

There is a time to take counsel of your fears, and there is a time never to listen to any fear.
George S. Patton

Self-confidence is crucial in almost every aspect of our lives, so spend some time thinking about what it is, and how to get it.

Pride is the mask
of one's own faults.
Jewish proverb

**The way you
overcome shyness
is to become so
wrapped up in
something that you
forget to be afraid.**
Lady Bird Johnson

Confidence is like a parachute. If it's carefully planned, prepared, and packed, it will open beautifully at the right time, allowing the bearer a great flight and a safe landing.

Do what you believe to be right, whatever other people think. Ignoring mockery and criticism, and confidently following your own path, is a sign of your integrity, and in time, you will be respected for it.

Keep your fears to yourself but share your courage with others.
Robert Louis Stevenson

What have you achieved so far? List what you've done, and look at it often… it will help you remember how far you've come.

Prepare yourself for success.
That way, you'll have more
chance of succeeding!

Envy is a waste of time.

There are very few monsters who warrant the fear we have of them. *André Gide*

No one is as angry as the person who is wrong.

To conquer fear is the beginning of wisdom.
Bertrand Russell

Leadership is about people looking at you and gaining confidence. If you feel in control, then they will, too.

If you work hard, and try to learn, you'll make progress; and if you make progress, it will build your confidence.

Who is more foolish, the child afraid of the dark, or the man afraid of the light?
Maurice Freehill

Footprints on the sands of time
are not made by sitting down.

Every time you look fear in the face, you gain another rung on the ladder of confidence.

Carry yourself with dignity and grace; try to make others feel relaxed and comfortable; be observant; and you may, as well as giving the impression that you are confident, become so.

Life is so much easier when
you feel good about yourself
– your talents, your abilities,
and your relationships
with others.

Life shrinks or expands in proportion to one's courage.

Confidence comes, not from always being right, but from not fearing to be wrong.

Promise yourself that you will continue on your lifelong journey to confidence, come what may, and that you will never let yourself down.

If a goal is worth achieving, it's worth waiting for. Confidence gives you the patience to hold out for your dreams.

A beautiful day as you set out on your journey: the sun shining, the birds singing, a cloudless sky… what could be a greater confidence booster than that? And it's all completely free!

Imagine yourself as a successful person – what you'd wear, how you'd behave, the work you'd do. Then work towards that … it may not be so very far off!

Confidence breeds confidence.

If you want to be trusted, first trust yourself.

Confidence is like a passport or an identity card. If you don't have it, you'll be lost, and you won't be able to travel forward on your journey.

Confidence is the key. So open up!

If the young knew, and the old could, there's nothing that couldn't be done.

To win the crown
Never back down!

Don't extol your own virtues; wait for others to do that for you! Boasting is a sign that you may be lacking in self-confidence, and need to constantly remind others of your achievements.

The purpose of life is to live it, to taste experience to the utmost, to reach out eagerly and without fear for newer and richer experience. *Eleanor Roosevelt*

Why be optimistic?
Well… why not?!

Forget what others think of you. Confidence is about what you think of yourself.

The moment you start to compare yourself to others is the moment you start to lose confidence in yourself.

Some of us are born confident; some learn it from the love and care they experience when they're growing up; and some have to seek it for ourselves, not knowing where we may find it but having faith that we will.

Experience is not what happens to a man; it is what a man does with what happens to him.
Aldous Huxley

Feed your faith and your fear will starve to death.

Confidence is knowing that you are loved and valued – and being able to love and value those around you.

Confess you were wrong yesterday; it will show you are wise today.

Tough times don't last; tough people do.

Self confidence is what brings us integrity, the ability to live our lives according to a set of values that we believe in, whatever those around us may think of us.

I have accepted fear as a part of life – specifically, the fear of change… I have gone ahead despite the pounding in the heart that says: turn back.
Erica Jong

If you feel confident in yourself, you will find that you have no need to boast.

Life is pleasant. Death is peaceful. It's the transition that's troublesome.
Isaac Asimov

You cannot acquire experience by making experiments. You cannot create experience. You must undergo it. ***Albert Camus***

Some people tell themselves everything will go wrong so that they'll avoid disappointment. But this kind of negative attitude can be a self-fulfilling prophecy; if you always predict doom and gloom, the chances are that you'll miss out on opportunities, and then you won't achieve the kind of success you'd been secretly hoping for.

Try to live the life you have imagined; then it may come closer to being a reality.

There is no cure for birth and death save to enjoy the interval. *George Santayana*

If what you have done yesterday still looks big to you, you cannot have done much today. *Mikhail Gorbachev*

Don't lie about your failures in the past, but don't dwell on them, either. Unless they're relevant to the discussion in hand, there's no need to bring them up, especially to people who hardly know you.

Old age is not for the faint-hearted.

Confidence in the face of loss is the greatest confidence of all.

From all that I saw
And everywhere I wandered
I learned that time cannot be spent
It can only be squandered.
Roman Payne

Confidence, or lack of it, shows in your face. Look at the photos of yourself taken over the years… can you tell, behind the smiles for the camera, when you were at your most happy and confident?

Confidence is not a way of avoiding difficulty, but of dealing with it when it comes.

Procrastination, putting things off until tomorrow, may be a sign that you lack confidence to fulfil your dreams. Perhaps if you make your dreams a little more realistic, you can start doing something to make them come true today.

If you think you are beaten, you are;
If you think you dare not, you don't.
If you'd like to win, but think you can't
It's almost a cinch you won't.
Walter D. Wintle

One of the ways to give a child confidence is to show them how much you like them, as well as how much you love them. Being happy to see a child, and showing the pleasure you take in their existence, is the biggest confidence boost you can offer.

Almost everyone appreciates a compliment, as long as it's sincere. So spread a little confidence by being positive about other people's talents and skills whenever you can.

No one is supremely confident, however much they may appear so. We are all human beings with faults and weaknesses that worry and frighten us. So remember that when you're dealing with people who intimidate you; it might help to make you feel more confident yourself.

Confidence is going after Moby Dick in a rowboat and taking the tartar sauce with you. *Zig Ziglar*

You make a story of your life as you go along. Let it be a truthful one, but also a positive one. For your achievements are much more interesting than your failures!

Don't forget to take your Vitamin C pill every day: and with it, a large dose of courage, commitment, and confidence!

If at first you don't succeed, you're doing it wrong. Learn from the experience. Try again, but with a different approach. *Steve Maraboli*

The good traveller is a confident person, able to enjoy many different kinds of people, surroundings and situations, and to stay calm and even-tempered, even when plans go awry.

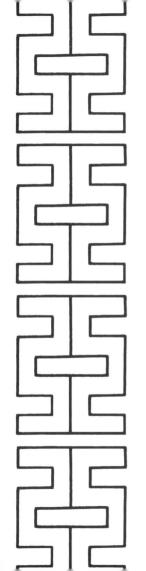

Taking your first steps; riding your first bike; learning to swim, read, dance, play the piano… Little by little, that's how you gained your confidence in life.

Confidence is not a matter of mindless optimism. It is, rather, a positive assessment of our talents, skills, and strengths, and a desire to make the most of them.

293

Guilt has its place in life; if you do something wrong, you should show remorse. But don't allow it to overshadow your life; pay your dues, and move on with confidence.

Don't make excuses for your mistakes. Own up, and show that you have the confidence to take responsibility for what you've done.

Don't generalize. Just because you had a bad day yesterday, doesn't mean you'll have one tomorrow.

If we did all the things we are capable of, we would astound ourselves. *Thomas Edison*

Inaction breeds doubt and fear. Action breeds confidence and courage. If you want to conquer fear, do not sit home and think about it. Go out and get busy.

Dale Carnegie

When you make a mistake, don't start to believe that it is a bad omen, a sign that you will make many more. Recognize it for what it is, and move on.

Confidence: self-knowledge; self-esteem; self-respect. Lack of confidence: self-consciousness; self-hatred; self-pity.

Smile, laugh, love…
be confident.

Knowing that someone loves you, passionately and devotedly, is a wonderful cure for low self-confidence. All at once, you will feel clever, beautiful, fascinating. And it can happen overnight!

Sometimes, you need to swim against the tide. For that, you need confidence. And when at last you reach the shore, you'll find you've gained more confidence on the way.

For a man, putting on a suit and tie can inspire confidence. For a woman, a formal evening dress, glittering jewellery, and beautiful shoes. If you look like a million dollars, it won't be long before you start to feel it, too!

299

Have you ever really asked yourself the question, 'Who am I'? It takes confidence to do so. And more confidence, of course, to answer it!

People who give us their full confidence believe that they have thereby earned the right to ours. This is a fallacy; one does not acquire rights through gifts.

Friedrich Nietzsche

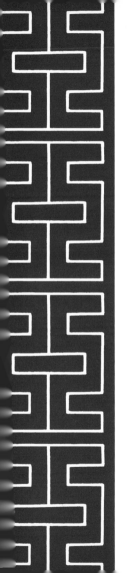

Each human being on the planet is a complex mix of emotions: of self-confidence and fear; of love and anger; of joy and despair. Try to understand how these fleeting moods compete within them, not only in the people you love, but in the faces of strangers.

**If it is to be
It is up to me.**

Every day do something that will inch you closer to a better tomorrow. *Doug Firebaugh*

When you speak to people, look them confidently in the eye. Even if you are shy, show them that you are not afraid of them, and that you are not ashamed of yourself.

Confidence grows with age. As we get older, we become less and less inclined to change so as to blend in with the people around us. We become more 'ourselves' – for better or for worse!

The only journey is the journey within.
Rainer Maria Rilke

Parting from a loved one is easier if we feel confident that our relationship will survive the absence – and may, indeed, grow stronger.

The greatest part of confidence is the will to get things done, and the energy to do them.

Modesty and confidence
are natural partners.

Doubt is not always a sign of weakness. In many cases, it leads us to question what we know, and find out more about the world we live in.

Those who whistle in the dark help to keep their spirits up.

You have been told that, even like a chain, you are as weak as your weakest link. This is but half the truth. You are also as strong as your strongest link. To measure you by your smallest deed is to reckon the power of the ocean by the frailty of its foam. To judge you by your failures is to cast blame upon the seasons for their inconstancy.
Khalil Gibran

If you are not confident in an obvious way, don't pretend to be. Instead, let your inner strength of character show to people who are discerning and sensitive enough to notice it.

Confidence can be a pose; but if it's only skin deep, you will soon be found out.

We do not change as we grow older. We just become more clearly ourselves. *Lynn Hall*

Follow your honest convictions, and stay strong.

William Thackeray

Do not be afraid to travel slowly; only be afraid to stand still. **Chinese proverb**

Insist on yourself. Never imitate.

Ralph Waldo Emerson

Being direct and honest is a quality that most people value highly in life. Sometimes, saying clearly exactly what you want avoids a lot of time, trouble, and misunderstanding. And it's not selfish, as long as you are not hurting anyone else's feelings, or disregarding their needs; it simply shows you have confidence.

Confidence: preparation, application, determination... and perspiration!

You can only become what you are by refusing to be what others have decided you should be.

Everybody wants to be confident, but there are no short cuts. Confidence comes through hard work, testing yourself, and not being afraid to fail.

'Black-and-white thinking' is the enemy of confidence. Boundless optimism when things go well is replaced by darkest despair when the smallest hitch is encountered. Instead, cultivate a philosophical attitude. The likeliest eventuality is that most things will go right, but some things will go wrong.

If you look at a beautiful woman and
envy her confident, carefree manner,
rest assured that you do not know the
whole picture. Her history and present
circumstances, her joys and sorrow, may
not be at all as you imagine.

When you look in the mirror every morning, tell yourself: I am a confident person. After a while, you will find yourself closer to being one.

If your confidence is low, ask yourself, what is so bad about me? I'm just a human being, like any other, with strengths and weaknesses. Why should I be so down on myself?

Planting bulbs for spring is an expression of confidence. We can't be sure that they'll come up, but we do our best, adding grit to the soil to prevent them rotting in the ground, and compost to help them grow. Then we wait, hoping to see them bloom in all their glory, once the dark days are past.

Being an individual can be hard when you're young; as you get older, you get to know yourself better, and don't mind standing out from the crowd.

Sometimes, we minimize our achievements in the hope that others will not be jealous of us. That's not the right strategy. Instead, be proud of yourself, and learn to take compliments gracefully.

Wait for others to tell you you've done well. It will feel better than prompting them to do so by boasting about your achievements.

315

Confidence doesn't just happen. You will only find it by setting yourself goals, whether small or large, and working until you achieve them… which will give you the biggest confidence boost you could hope for.

Train your talents; select your skills; work on your weaknesses. That way lies confidence.

What does life expect from you? And what do you expect from life? Begin by asking these questions, and then set about answering them.

Clearing your mind of all thoughts, worries, and plans, and simply being present in the moment, just for a few minutes every day, can bring a new sense of calmness and confidence into your life.

Believe you are powerful
Believe you are strong
Believe you can achieve your goals
Believe in the promise of tomorrow
Believe you can fulfil your dreams
Believe in yourself.

If you do well in life, there are always going to be people who are jealous of you. Don't blame yourself, or them, for what is an entirely human emotion; simply recognize the situation, and try to rise above it.

Under-confidence is sometimes a form of egocentric behaviour. People with low self-esteem constantly think about themselves, and how they compare to those around them. Instead of reassuring others, they need constant reassurance themselves.

All of us feel insecure sometimes. It's important to recognize that, both in ourselves and in others, but not to let it overshadow our enjoyment of life.

Fight the Fear

The biggest block to self-confidence is fear, which can manifest itself in many ways: worrying too much what others may think of us, being afraid to fail, and so on. Once again, taking a fresh look at what bothers us may be the key to allowing ourselves the freedom to move forward.

He who fears to suffer, suffers from fear.

Where does confidence comes from? Not from having no fear, but from refusing to be intimidated by fear.

The curious person, who is always interested in learning about the world, often forgets to be afraid.

The basis of hatred between people is fear. Fear of the unknown, of the different. The basis of love is a sense of confidence that we all share one common humanity.

If you fear something, you give it power to rule your life.

Who sees all beings in his own self, and his own self in all beings, loses his fear. *Upanishads*

We learn fear as we grow up. In some ways, that will protect us through life, making sure we do not do foolish things. But it can also limit our possibilities, if we become afraid of taking any kind of risk at all.

If we are too afraid of failing, we will never find the confidence to succeed.

In skating over thin ice, our safety is in our speed.

Ralph Waldo Emerson

Trying to avoid risk at all times is a sign of a lack of confidence. And it doesn't work. Life is a risky business, and the more security you crave, the more frightened you will be of that fact.

Facing your fears is the best way to become strong, courageous, confident, and successful.

'Well done': two words that build confidence. Use them whenever you can, and listen with pride when they're applied to you.

Where no hope is left,
is left no fear. *Milton*

Bring a child up to respect authority, not be afraid of it. That way, you instil confidence from the beginning.

There is no choice but to go forward. If you are afraid, and don't have the confidence to face the challenges of life, you can be sure you will start to go backwards.

Confidence: when faith is greater than fear.

There's never a time that we can say that from all points of view, we are secure. Life has a way of springing surprises on us, bad and good. Our task is to meet those challenges with confidence, not to wish them away.

Have you tried listing your fears and insecurities? If so, you'll know that, when they're written down, some of them look pretty silly!

Make confidence a habit: instead of saying, no, I can't, say, yes I can. Instead of thinking, nothing will ever go right, think instead, I'm sure this will work out. After a while, you'll find your bad habit – of negativity – has become a good one – of confidence.

To me, faith means not worrying. *John Dewey*

Doubt is a pain too lonely to know that faith is his twin brother.
Khalil Gibran

When you look back on your life, do you find that you spent more time worrying than was necessary? That you could have been more confident? If so, make a resolution: don't worry so much in future.

Confidence brings inner tranquillity. Only when we stop worrying, and are present in the moment, can we take pleasure in the beauty of the world around us, and find the mental concentration to focus on each detail of it.

As confidence grows, so too do the possibilities we see for ourselves in the future.

If you see ten troubles coming down the road, you can be sure that nine will run into the ditch before they meet you. *Calvin Coolidge*

How much pain they have cost us, the evils which never happened. *Thomas Jefferson*

Set out on the path to confidence. Just making that decision is a sign of confidence in itself, and bodes well for your journey.

Fight your fears as if they were fleas – a nuisance, nothing more.

If you're busy in the daytime, and fall in to bed exhausted at night, there's a chance you won't have time to worry.

'Hey, you!' Do you shrink when you hear someone address you like that, fearing you've done something wrong? Or do you turn to see who's calling you, an expression of amused curiosity on your face?

Aim low, and you are sure to hit your mark. Aim high, and you may miss it. But whatever happens, you are sure to experience a greater sense of achievement than if you simply stay within what you consider are your limitations.

Take notice of the good things about yourself. Let others notice the bad.

When you find confidence, you will look at the world and wonder why you ever felt afraid.

For most of us, confidence does not just arrive. You have to find it, and renew your quest at the beginning of every day.

Have a song to sing. And sing that song out loud and clear, with confidence.

Don't envy a person's 'natural' confidence. Chances are, you don't know the intimate details of his or her life. That confidence may have been hard won, through trials and tribulations that no one would want to endure.

If you live up to your own expectations, you'll find yourself living up to the expectations of those around you.

A faith is a necessity to a man.
Woe to him who believes in nothing.
Victor Hugo

Be faithful in small things, because
it is in them that your faith lies.
Mother Teresa

On life's path, light your way by
wisdom, trying to take each challenge
as it comes, and doing your best
to face it with thought, care, and
determination. Confidence will follow,
as the day the night.

Having a pleasant, tolerant attitude will get you a long way in life. Don't underestimate the importance of being nice to people – it's a sign that you're confident, and can think of others, not just yourself.

Faith consists in believing when it is beyond the power of reason to believe. *Voltaire*

Worrying is hard work. Give yourself a break. Tell yourself you'll come back to that worry later, and then forget to do so!

The most basic of all human wishes is to find a meaning in life. Be confident that you can, and you will.

Fear is a response to an immediate danger; anxiety is focused on a future one, which is not always as clear as we'd like it to be. We sometimes need fear, in order to protect ourselves; we very seldom need anxiety.

Anxiety is fear without an object.

When you try to comfort a friend in difficulty, you tell them, 'It will be OK', not 'Oh dear, this is terrible, and it might get even worse'. Treat yourself in the same way. You deserve the same kindness to yourself as you give to your friends.

Faith in oneself is the best and safest course. *Michaelangelo*

Faith is taking the first step, even when you can't see the whole staircase. *Martin Luther King*

Be creative; accept responsibility; choose your path. Only in this way will you learn to challenge the feelings of anxiety that are part of our natural response to the human condition in which we find ourselves: that we live, we die, and we don't know why.

Don't dwell on negative consequences. Worry less about failure, or the disapproval of others. Think, instead, about the task at hand: how best you can achieve it.

Confidence can be a self-fulfilling prophecy: those who have confidence may succeed because they think they will, while those who lack it may fail because they expect to.

Self-confidence doesn't come from nowhere. It is something we learn, through the experience of completing tasks successfully, through hard work, patience, and determination.

Optimism is the faith that leads to achievement. Nothing can be done without hope and confidence.

Helen Keller

Confidence: being certain about a chosen course of action.
Self-confidence: having the belief in oneself necessary to pursue it.

Faith is an end, not a beginning.

Some kinds of fear are very important. Without them, we'd take all manner of careless risks, endangering our lives. But some are irrational, and serve only to prevent us from living as freely, and fully, as we'd like to.

Achieving
Your Goal

We all need a sense of purpose in life, but our aims are not all the same, by any means. Setting your own goals, and working to achieve them in your own way, at your own pace, is part of being confident in yourself, and showing the way forward to others, too.

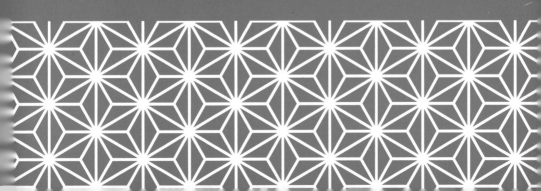

A purpose, goal, or aim, is essential to most people in life. It can be great or small… but it has to be there.

Perfectionism is the enemy of confidence.

Set your goal; set your schedule; set your deadline; and then set your leisure time!

Once you choose hope, anything is possible. *Christopher Reeve*

Ask yourself, what is my personal goal? You won't be able to achieve it unless you know what it is. And you won't know what it is until you sit down and really think about what matters to you, and what kind of difference you want to make.

Long-term goals depend on short-term achievements.

Don't listen to that inner voice that tells you, You Can't. To achieve any kind of goal, you must believe that You Can.

Goals don't have to be all about work. Your goal could easily be, to spend more time doing what you enjoy, whether that's with your family and friends, or pursuing some creative task, sport, or hobby.

The question isn't who is going to let me; it's who is going to stop me. *Ayn Rand*

We all have a lot of goals in life. The trick is to know how to prioritize them, and how to have the confidence to stick to our decision.

We know our limitations only too well. But that should not stop us from trying to exceed them.

If we believe that things will turn out well in the end, we make it more likely that they will.

The best angle to approach any problem in life is the try-angle.

Obstacles are those frightful things you see when you take your eyes off your goal. *Henry Ford*

Turn your face to the sun so that the shadows fall behind you. *Māori proverb*

Our dreams are always a size too big, so we can grow into them.

Inspiration is the first step on the route to achievement; confidence the second; determination the third; patience the fourth; and perseverance the fifth.

It is not position, but disposition, that makes a person confident.

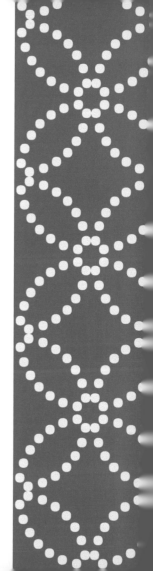

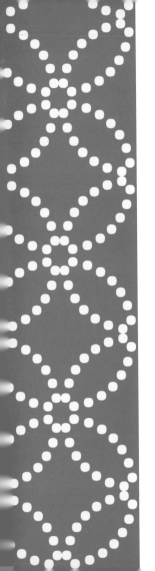

It is easier to go down a hill than up, but the best view is from the top.
Arnold Bennett

Motivation is when your dreams put on their work clothes.

Happiness lies in the joy of achievement and the thrill of creative effort.
Franklin D. Roosevelt

The greatest discovery of my generation is that a human being can alter his life by altering his attitudes.
William James

If someone is rude to you, you may think to yourself, 'That person hates me, nobody likes me'; or you may turn the situation round, and say 'I wonder what's the matter with old so-and-so today? Why's he in such a grumpy mood?'

Happiness and confidence go hand in hand.
When I feel happy, I feel confident that I can do
anything. When I feel confident that I can do
anything, I feel happy.

People often feel they should keep their
problems to themselves. Don't. Tell
people you love and trust about your
worries; with a good support system
behind you, you'll find you can begin to
deal with whatever life throws at you.

I attempt a difficult task; but there is no worth in that which is not a difficult achievement. *Ovid*

Those with confidence find they can achieve in life, and their achievements then go on to add to their confidence; while those without it suffer from perceived failures, which in turn damage their confidence.

It seems to me we can never give up longing and wishing while we are thoroughly alive. There are certain things we feel to be beautiful and good, and we must hunger after them. *George Eliot*

Being able to disagree politely, but firmly, is one of the most important social skills we can learn.

If you're not confident, act as though you are. People may not notice the difference.

We would all like an easy life, but if we got it, we'd find it lacked the kind of challenges that bring us alive, move us on, make us hungry for achievement, and give us a sense of purpose.

If you fear making anyone mad, then you ultimately probe for the lowest common denominator of human achievement.
Jimmy Carter

Ask for what you're entitled to; only after you've been told you can't have it, need you demand.

Ah, but a man's reach should exceed his grasp Or what's a heaven for?
Robert Browning

What is a confident person? Someone who is not ashamed to speak up; not afraid to rise to life's challenges; able to continue working towards a goal, whatever the difficulties; courageous enough to go it alone when circumstances demand; and with a strong sense of moral integrity.

Think about what makes you feel confident, and what makes you feel anxious. Then consciously seek out those situations where you feel more yourself, and at ease.

Until you put your mind to achieving your aim, there is little chance that you will reach your goal.

A confidence trick occurs when a swindler wins your confidence… and then your money!

Set goals high enough to inspire you; and low enough to encourage you.

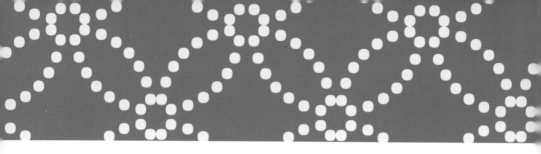

Beautiful people are not necessarily more confident than others. In fact, they may suffer from an anxiety that they must always appear looking their best, and that others may cease to value them if they do not.

Goals that are not written down are merely wishes.

**If you don't know where you're going,
you'll probably end up somewhere else.**
Lewis Carroll

To achieve your
dreams, you must
first convert them
into goals.

They say it's lonely at the top. Maybe that's because once you get there, you find that you still need what you had when you were on the way up – a purpose for living.

Is confidence an innate quality, or something that we learn? Nobody knows, but it seems that, for most of us, it's a combination of the two.

Suspend your disbelief: tell yourself that you'll be able to achieve your aims, and then you will.

Age may make our bodies weak; but it makes our minds strong, as the wisdom that comes with experience gives us confidence to live our lives as we want to.

If you have built castles in the air, your work need not be lost; that is where they should be. Now put foundations under them. *Henry David Thoreau*

Be thine own palace, or the world's thy jail.

John Donne

Athletes spend many years training so that they can do their best. The same is true of life: you need to train yourself to be confident.

The only race worth winning is the one against yourself.

Creativity is a great motivator because it makes people interested in what they are doing. Creativity gives hope that there can be a worthwhile idea. Creativity gives the possibility of some sort of achievement to everyone. Creativity makes life more fun and more interesting. *Edward de Bono*

In order to achieve a goal, we often have to sacrifice immediate pleasures. However, that shouldn't mean that we become obsessive. A confident outlook is one in which all aspects of life, whether work or leisure-oriented, have their place.

Instead of going over your mistakes, try learning from them. Then you can forget them, because they'll be of no use any more.

Life isn't all about achieving your goals. It's about wanting to achieve them.

All of us are confident in some way: our life's task is to find that way, and from there, take the first steps to being confident in every way.

Children learn confidence from their parents; adults from themselves.

Confidence is elusive. It is aligned to faith, but it is not faith; to hope, but it is not hope; to love, but it is not love. Perhaps it is a dash of each of these: faith, hope, love, and the will to make them matter.

Allow yourself time to live, whether it's walking in the fresh air, feeling the warm sun on your shoulders, or gazing up at the stars. That way, you'll begin to forget about your worries and live confidently, in the moment.

Our greatest achievement lies in how to love, and be loved in return.

Fair play, not competitiveness; kindness, not selfishness: these are the marks of true confidence.

A man should have any number of little aims about which he should be conscious and for which he should have names, but he should have neither name for nor consciousness concerning the main aim of his life. *Samuel Butler*

Sometimes it pays to take a step back from your life and ask yourself, what am I really trying to achieve here? Having the confidence to review your life choices from time to time is part of building a secure, stable sense of your own identity.